DILIGENT HANDS

The plans of the Diligent lead to Profit

LESTER MULLER

CONTENTS

Introduction

Chapter 1: Laziness

1. The consequences of Laziness
2. Struggling with Laziness
3. Effects of Laziness on personal life & case study

Chapter 2: Diligent Hands

1. The rewards of Diligence
2. Benefits of hard work and determination
3. Inspiring story of J.K. Rowling

Chapter 3: Building Diligent Habits

1. Practical advice on developing a strong work ethic
2. Strategies for overcoming procrastination and staying motivated

Chapter 4: Navigating Challenges and Setbacks

1. Learning from failures and using them as opportunities for growth
2. Developing resilience and perseverance

Chapter 5: Cultivating a Diligent Mindset

1. Understanding and developing a Diligent Mindset
2. Practicing Self-Discipline and Self-Awareness

INTRODUCTION

Diligence is the steady, intentional pursuit of excellence through focused effort and perseverance. It goes beyond simply working hard; it's about maintaining commitment to your goals, even when faced with difficulties or distractions. A diligent person consistently takes purposeful steps toward improvement, understanding that success is built through small, incremental actions over time. Whether in academics, personal development, or professional life, diligence helps transform aspirations into achievements. By fostering a mindset of persistence and attention to detail, we cultivate the discipline needed to overcome challenges and achieve lasting results. Diligence, in essence, is the driving force behind sustained progress and growth.

CHAPTER I
LAZINESS

1. The Consequences of Laziness

Laziness, often defined as the unwillingness to exert effort, is a universal trait that everyone experiences at some point. While it might seem harmless when it manifests in short bursts, laziness can have far-reaching consequences when it becomes a persistent habit. The impacts of laziness can affect individuals both personally and their loved ones, professionally and their colleges, creating a domino effect that impairs growth, development, and overall well-being.

One of the primary consequences of laziness is procrastination. Yes, you heard me. When individuals avoid tasks due to a lack of motivation, they often fall behind on responsibilities. This can lead to missed deadlines, reduced productivity, and diminished quality of work. I've experienced this in my own workplace after I suffered memory loss due to Covid19. Over time, this can result in a loss of opportunities, especially in professional settings where consistent performance is expected. If left unchecked, laziness can create a cycle of missed opportunities, diminishing confidence and ambition, making it increasingly difficult for a person to achieve their goals.

CHAPTER I
LAZINESS

Laziness also contributes to a deterioration in mental and physical health. Physically, inactivity leads to weight gain, weakened muscles, and increased risk of chronic illnesses like heart disease, diabetes, and obesity. Mentally,the worse laziness, can result in feelings of guilt, anxiety, and depression, especially when tasks pile up and seem insurmountable. The stress of avoiding responsibilities can compound over time, creating emotional distress and a feeling of being trapped in one's own unproductive habits.

In relationships, laziness can cause tension and dissatisfaction. When individuals fail to contribute to household responsibilities or social obligations, it can lead to resentment from family members, friends, and colleagues. Over time, this erodes trust and damages personal connections. Professionally, laziness might lead to a reputation for being unreliable or unmotivated, affecting career progression and peer relationships.

Furthermore, **laziness stifles personal growth**. The act of avoiding challenges or difficult tasks prevents individuals from developing critical skills, knowledge, and resilience. People who consistently avoid effort fail to experience the learning curve associated with overcoming obstacles. This can stifle creativity, critical thinking, and adaptability, all of which are necessary for success in an ever-evolving world.

CHAPTER I
LAZINESS

Ultimately, laziness can trap individuals in a state of mediocrity. When people allow laziness to dictate their actions, they often settle for less, opting for immediate gratification over long-term success. This limits their potential, causing them to miss out on life experiences that require discipline and perseverance.

2. Struggling with Laziness

The struggle with laziness is one that affects nearly everyone at some point. Even highly motivated individuals may find themselves succumbing to bouts of laziness, unable to muster the energy to complete tasks. Understanding the reasons behind this struggle can help address the issue more effectively.

One common cause of laziness is overwhelm. When people face a large or daunting task, the sheer size of the responsibility can feel paralyzing. Instead of breaking the task down into manageable steps which most of us don't do, the mind often shuts down, resulting in procrastination or avoidance. Sounds familiar? For instance, a student assigned a long research paper might feel overwhelmed by the scope of the project and decide to avoid it altogether, pushing the work off until the last minute. We all know, last minute results produce little to no effect. Let's dive deeper.

CHAPTER I
LAZINESS

Mental health can also play a significant role in the struggle with laziness. Conditions like depression, anxiety, and burnout can sap an individual energy, making it difficult to engage with tasks, no matter how small. In these cases, laziness is more than just a lack of willpower — it's a symptom of deeper emotional or psychological struggles. For example, a person with depression may find it impossible to complete even simple tasks, not because they are lazy by nature, but because they are weighed down by their mental state. **"AS A MAN THINKETH, SO IS HE".**

Another factor is the influence of instant gratification. In today's fast-paced world, people are accustomed to receiving quick rewards for their efforts. When the rewards for a particular task are delayed, individuals are more likely to avoid the task, seeking activities that provide immediate satisfaction, such as browsing social media or watching TV. **The ease of access to distractions makes it harder to focus on tasks that require sustained effort.**

CHAPTER I
LAZINESS

Habits and environment also play significant roles in laziness. People who live in environments that promote laziness, such as cluttered or unorganized spaces, are more likely to struggle with maintaining motivation. Similarly, individuals who have developed poor time management habits may find themselves struggling to stay on top of their responsibilities. **Without structure, it becomes easier to give into laziness.**

Struggling with laziness often leads to feelings of guilt and frustration. Many individuals feel disappointed in themselves when they fail to complete tasks, which can lead to a vicious cycle of avoidance. **The key to overcoming laziness lies in self-awareness and actionable strategies.** Recognizing the underlying causes, whether they be psychological, environmental, or motivational, allows individuals to address the root problem rather than merely trying to push through with brute force.

CHAPTER I
LAZINESS

3. The Effects of Laziness on Personal and Professional Life & Case Study

Laziness has profound effects on both personal and professional life, often limiting opportunities for success and fulfillment. **On a personal level, laziness can hinder the ability to pursue goals and develop healthy habits.** Individuals who struggle with consistent laziness may find themselves neglecting important aspects of life such as exercise, self-care, and meaningful relationships. Over time, this can lead to a sense of dissatisfaction with one's personal life, as they fail to achieve the milestones they desire, whether it be in terms of health, hobbies, or family.

For instance, someone who dreams of writing a novel but consistently avoids working on their craft may look back years later and regret the time lost to procrastination. Similarly, laziness can prevent individuals from taking care of their health, leading to poor physical condition and diminished quality of life.

CHAPTER I
LAZINESS

In professional settings, laziness is particularly damaging. Productivity, efficiency, and reliability are key traits that employers value. An individual who consistently exhibits lazy behavior, such as missing deadlines, avoiding responsibilities, or producing subpar work, risks stagnating in their career or even losing their job. In professions that require continuous learning and skill development, laziness can prevent individuals from staying competitive. For example, in the fast-evolving tech industry, failing to keep up with the latest developments due to laziness can result in a rapid decline in career prospects.

Moreover, laziness in the workplace can harm relationships with colleagues. Teamwork and collaboration are essential in most professional environments, and someone who does not contribute equally to group efforts can strain relationships with peers. This can lead to a loss of trust and respect from colleagues, which may further isolate the individual and create an unsupportive work environment.

CHAPTER I
LAZINESS
3.1. Case Study: John's Struggle with Laziness

John, a 32-year-old graphic designer, had always been passionate about art. However, over time, he developed a habit of procrastinating on his projects. Initially, this started as a minor issue, with John missing a few deadlines but catching up soon after. However, as the workload increased, so did John's laziness. He began to avoid tasks altogether, often binge-watching television shows or playing video games instead of working on his designs.

John's laziness had severe consequences on both his personal and professional life. In his personal life, he became distant from friends and family, choosing to stay home and avoid social gatherings. His health deteriorated as he neglected exercise and healthy eating. Professionally, his clients grew increasingly dissatisfied with his missed deadlines and low-quality work, leading to a loss of business.

Eventually, John's employer had to intervene. After being confronted by his boss, John realized that his laziness was costing him both his career and his well-being. He sought help from a coach who helped him create a structured plan for managing his tasks. Through this plan, John started setting small, achievable goals each day, which helped him overcome his initial feelings of overwhelm. He also made an effort to declutter his workspace and eliminate distractions, allowing him to focus more effectively on his work.

CHAPTER I
LAZINESS

Eventually, John's employer had to intervene. After being confronted by his boss, John realized that his laziness was costing him both his career and his well-being. He sought help from a coach who helped him create a structured plan for managing his tasks. Through this plan, John started setting small, achievable goals each day, which helped him overcome his initial feelings of overwhelm. He also made an effort to declutter his workspace and eliminate distractions, allowing him to focus more effectively on his work.

Over time, John's performance improved, and he was able to regain the trust of his clients. His personal life also improved as he reconnected with friends and family, becoming more engaged in social activities. This case illustrates how laziness, when left unchecked, can spiral into significant personal and professional challenges, but with the right strategies and mindset, it is possible to overcome it and regain control over one's life.

CHAPTER II
DILIGENT HANDS
THE PLANS OF THE DILIGENT LEAD TO PROFIT

1. The Rewards of Diligence

Diligence, the quality of being careful and persistent in one's work, is often regarded as one of the most critical traits for success in any field. It involves consistent effort, patience, and the ability to push through obstacles, regardless of how challenging the task may be. While natural talent or intelligence can be beneficial, it is diligence that often distinguishes those who achieve long-term success from those who merely coast on short-lived talent.

One of the primary rewards of diligence is mastery. When individuals approach tasks with persistence and a strong work ethic, they are more likely to develop a deep understanding of their craft. This kind of expertise only comes with time, repeated practice, and learning from mistakes. My Regional Manager once said, **"when we fail, we fail forward"**, those words resonate with me. For example, could be seen in the story of Thomas Edison and his invention of the light bulb. Edison failed thousands of times before successfully creating a functional light bulb. Instead of viewing these failures as setbacks, he saw each one as a step closer to success. After each attempt, he learned what didn't work, adjusting his approach until he eventually found the right formula.

CHAPTER II
DILIGENT HANDS
THE PLANS OF THE DILIGENT LEAD TO PROFIT

Edison famously said, "I have not failed. I've just found 10,000 ways that won't work." His mindset illustrates how failing forward works: each failure brought him closer to his goal by providing valuable lessons, ultimately leading to a breakthrough. This shows that failure, when approached with the right mindset, can propel us toward success, making each misstep a necessary part of the journey. Diligence cultivates mastery, which in turn leads to personal satisfaction and recognition from others.

Another reward of diligence is the development of resilience. Life is full of challenges, and those who face setbacks and difficulties with diligence tend to bounce back stronger than before. This persistence builds mental toughness and a can-do attitude. Rather than being discouraged by failure, diligent individuals view setbacks as opportunities to learn and improve. **Over time, they develop the resilience needed to handle even greater challenges with confidence.** In contrast, those who lack diligence may give up at the first sign of difficulty, missing out on the growth that comes from perseverance.

CHAPTER II
DILIGENT HANDS
THE PLANS OF THE DILIGENT LEAD TO PROFIT

Diligence also brings a sense of fulfillment and purpose. Individuals who consistently apply themselves toward meaningful goals experience a sense of accomplishment when they see the fruits of their labor. Whether it's completing a difficult project at work, starting a business, or achieving personal goals, the satisfaction of reaching a target through hard work is unmatched. **It affirms the idea that the journey is just as important as the destination.** The discipline and commitment that come with diligence make the final achievement all the more rewarding because it represents a culmination of sustained effort.

Moreover, diligence often leads to greater opportunities in both personal and professional life. In the workplace, employees who consistently demonstrate diligence and reliability are more likely to be noticed by managers, supervisors and colleagues. This can lead to promotions, salary increases, and new responsibilities. **Employers value individuals who are not only skilled but also demonstrate a strong work ethic.** The trust built through consistent hard work opens doors for future success, whether through career advancement, networking opportunities, or even entrepreneurial ventures.

CHAPTER II
DILIGENT HANDS
THE PLANS OF THE DILIGENT LEAD TO PROFIT

Finally, diligence fosters personal growth. Through persistent effort, individuals learn to manage their time, set priorities, and balance short-term gratification with long-term rewards. They develop a strong sense of discipline, which spills over into other areas of life, from health and fitness to personal relationships. In many ways, diligence helps people build the habits and mindset necessary for a well-rounded and successful life.

2. Benefits of Hard work and Determination

Hard work and determination are foundational to success in almost every endeavor. While talent and intelligence are important, it is often the combination of grit and perseverance that yields the most significant results. **Hard work is the engine that drives progress, while determination keeps that engine running, even when the path to success becomes difficult or unclear.**

CHAPTER II
DILIGENT HANDS
THE PLANS OF THE DILIGENT LEAD TO PROFIT

One of the most notable benefits of hard work and determination is that they lead to tangible results. When individuals commit to putting in the necessary effort, they often achieve their goals, regardless of the obstacles that arise. This is because **hard work compounds over time** — each effort builds on the last, creating momentum that pushes individuals closer to their objectives. For instance, students who consistently study hard, even in subjects they find challenging, often perform better over time. Their determination to succeed and willingness to put in the necessary effort eventually pay off, leading to better grades and more opportunities for future success.

Hard work and determination also foster creativity and innovation. When people commit to a goal and are determined to achieve it, they are more likely to think creatively about how to overcome obstacles. **Problems that may have seemed insurmountable at first become solvable through perseverance and out-of-the-box thinking.** Determined individuals don't give up when faced with challenges; instead, they adapt and find new ways to move forward. This can be seen in entrepreneurs who, despite facing multiple business failures, continue to innovate and refine their ideas until they succeed. Their determination to overcome setbacks often leads to breakthroughs that would not have been possible without their hard work.

CHAPTER II
DILIGENT HANDS
THE PLANS OF THE DILIGENT LEAD TO PROFIT

In addition to personal achievements, hard work and determination build character. These qualities require individuals to push past comfort zones, embrace discipline, and cultivate patience. **Hard work instills a sense of responsibility, as individuals recognize that their actions have a direct impact on their success. Meanwhile, determination teaches the importance of persistence and focus, even in the face of adversity.** These traits are invaluable in life, as they help individuals navigate both personal and professional challenges with resilience and grace.

Another benefit of hard work and determination is their ability to inspire others. When individuals consistently put in the effort and stay committed to their goals, they set an example for those around them. Whether in a workplace, community, or family setting, the presence of a hard-working and determined individual often motivates others to raise their own standards. For example, in a team environment, a member who is determined to succeed can influence their peers to also put in their best efforts, creating a culture of collaboration and high performance.

CHAPTER II
DILIGENT HANDS
THE PLANS OF THE DILIGENT LEAD TO PROFIT

Finally, hard work and determination lead to self-confidence. When individuals see that their hard work leads to success, they gain confidence in their abilities. This self-assurance carries over into other areas of life, empowering them to take on new challenges with the belief that they can succeed through effort and perseverance. The process of working hard, learning from mistakes, and ultimately succeeding fosters a growth mindset, where individuals understand that they can always improve and achieve more with continued effort.

3. Inspiring Story: The Success of J.K. Rowling through Diligence and Determination

J.K. Rowling, the world-renowned author of the "Harry Potter" series, is a prime example of someone who attributes her success to diligence, hard work, and determination. Her story of overcoming adversity to achieve unprecedented success is both inspiring and a testament to the power of persistence.

CHAPTER II
DILIGENT HANDS
THE PLANS OF THE DILIGENT LEAD TO PROFIT

Before Rowling became a literary icon, she faced numerous personal and professional challenges. In the early 1990s, Rowling was a single mother living on welfare, struggling to make ends meet. She had just gone through a difficult divorce and was living in a small apartment in Edinburgh, Scotland, while trying to raise her daughter. Despite these hardships, Rowling remained determined to pursue her passion for writing.

Rowling's journey to success began when she conceived the idea for "Harry Potter" during a train ride. Inspired by the idea of a young boy discovering he was a wizard, she began writing the first novel of the series. However, her path was far from easy. Writing a novel while raising a child on a limited income required immense discipline and diligence. Rowling would often write in cafes while her daughter napped, dedicating every spare moment to working on the book.

CHAPTER II
DILIGENT HANDS
THE PLANS OF THE DILIGENT LEAD TO PROFIT

Despite her dedication, Rowling faced significant obstacles in getting her manuscript published. After completing the first "Harry Potter" book, she submitted it to multiple publishers, only to face repeated rejections. Twelve different publishing houses turned her down, each citing various reasons for why they believed the book would not be successful. Many aspiring authors would have given up after facing such constant rejection, but Rowling's determination kept her going. She believed in her story and was committed to finding a publisher who would see its potential.

Finally, after a year of trying, Bloomsbury Publishing accepted Rowling's manuscript. The first book in the "Harry Potter" series, "Harry Potter and the Philosopher's Stone," was published in 1997, and it quickly became a global sensation. Rowling's persistence and hard work paid off as the series grew into one of the most successful book franchises in history. Today, the "Harry Potter" books have sold over 500 million copies worldwide, and Rowling has become one of the wealthiest authors in the world.

CHAPTER II
DILIGENT HANDS
THE PLANS OF THE DILIGENT LEAD TO PROFIT

Rowling's success story is a powerful reminder that diligence and determination can help individuals overcome even the most difficult circumstances. Her ability to stay focused on her goals, despite personal and professional setbacks, demonstrates the value of perseverance. Through hard work and an unwavering belief in her abilities, Rowling was able to achieve her dreams and inspire millions of readers around the world.

Her story is not just about financial success but about the rewards of diligence. Rowling's dedication to her craft, her resilience in the face of rejection, and her determination to share her story with the world are what truly define her success. She remains an example of how hard work, determination, and a refusal to give up can lead to extraordinary achievements.

This story provide a comprehensive exploration of the rewards of diligence, the benefits of hard work and determination, and an inspiring case study of J.K. Rowling's success, which was rooted in these qualities. **Believe in yourself is your first step.**

CHAPTER III
BUILDING DILIGENT HABITS

1. Practical Advice on Developing a Strong Work Ethic

Developing a strong work ethic is essential for achieving success in both personal and professional life. A solid work ethic not only helps you complete tasks efficiently but also builds character, discipline, and a sense of responsibility. Here are some practical steps to cultivate a strong work ethic:
Set Clear Goals: Having specific, measurable, and achievable goals provides direction and purpose. When you know what you're working toward, it's easier to stay focused and motivated. Start by breaking down larger goals into smaller tasks that can be accomplished step by step. Each small victory will build momentum and keep you on track.

1.1 Prioritize Time Management: Time is one of your most valuable resources. Learning to manage it effectively is key to developing a strong work ethic. Create a daily or weekly schedule to allocate specific blocks of time for important tasks. Use tools like to-do lists, planners, or digital calendars to stay organized. Prioritize tasks based on importance and deadlines, tackling the most critical items first.

CHAPTER III
BUILDING DILIGENT HABITS

Commit to Consistency: A strong work ethic isn't built overnight; it comes from consistently showing up and putting in the effort, even when it's difficult. Establish routines that support your work habits, such as starting work at the same time every day or dedicating a few hours each evening to personal projects. The more consistent you are, the more likely you are to develop productive habits that contribute to long-term success.

Take Responsibility: Accountability is central to a strong work ethic. When you make a mistake or miss a deadline, own up to it even if it means you did bad. Focus on finding a solution rather than making excuses. **Taking responsibility shows integrity and fosters a growth mindset.** By learning from your mistakes, you'll become more resilient and better equipped to handle future challenges.

Embrace Challenges: A good work ethic involves pushing through difficulties and embracing challenges as opportunities for growth. Instead of avoiding difficult tasks, approach them with a problem-solving mindset. **Overcoming challenges builds confidence and demonstrates your willingness to put in the effort required to succeed.**

CHAPTER III
BUILDING DILIGENT HABITS

1.2 Maintain a Positive Attitude: A positive attitude can make a big difference in how you approach work. **Develop an I can attitude**, even when tasks seem tedious or overwhelming, staying optimistic will help you stay focused and productive. Cultivating gratitude for the opportunity to work and grow will also improve your outlook and help you push through difficult times.

1.3 Develop Self-Discipline: Self-discipline is the backbone of a strong work ethic. It's the ability to stay focused on your tasks without getting distracted or giving in to the temptation of procrastination. To build self-discipline, start by setting small, manageable goals that challenge you, but are attainable. Over time, increase the level of difficulty to gradually build your self-control.

Seek Continuous Improvement: A strong work ethic includes a commitment to ongoing learning and improvement. Whether through professional development courses, reading books, or learning from mentors, always look for ways to enhance your skills and knowledge. This dedication to growth will not only improve your work performance but also help you stay competitive in your field. I feel we going somewhere.

CHAPTER III
BUILDING DILIGENT HABITS

2. Strategies for Overcoming Procrastination and Staying Motivated

Procrastination can be one of the biggest roadblocks to productivity and maintaining a strong work ethic. Overcoming procrastination requires understanding its underlying causes and developing strategies to stay motivated and focused. Here are some practical tips to help you conquer procrastination and maintain motivation:

Identify the Root Cause of Procrastination: To effectively address procrastination, you need to understand why it's happening. Common reasons include fear of failure, feeling overwhelmed by a task, or a lack of clear direction. Once you identify the cause, you can develop specific strategies to overcome it. Do what works for you. For example, if you procrastinate because a task seems too large, break it down into smaller, more manageable steps.

Use the "Two-Minute Rule": A simple but powerful way to beat procrastination is to adopt the "Two-Minute Rule." If a task takes less than two minutes to complete, do it immediately. This helps you get started on small tasks, which can build momentum and make it easier to tackle larger tasks.

CHAPTER III
BUILDING DILIGENT HABITS

Break Tasks Into Smaller Chunks: One of the most effective ways to overcome procrastination is to break large tasks into smaller, more manageable parts. When a task feels overwhelming, it's easy to put it off. By dividing it into smaller sections, you make the task feel more approachable and easier to start. Completing one small section at a time builds a sense of accomplishment and motivates you to keep going.

Set Specific Deadlines: Without clear deadlines, tasks can drag on indefinitely. Set specific, realistic deadlines for yourself to create a sense of urgency and accountability. Publicly commit to your deadlines, whether by telling a colleague, friend, or even writing them down on a visible calendar. The more tangible your deadline, the more likely you are to stick to it.

Eliminate Distractions: Distractions are one of the biggest contributors to procrastination. Identify your biggest distractions — whether it's social media, TV, conversating to the same person or even minor tasks like organizing your workspace — and find ways to eliminate or minimize them. For instance, consider using apps that block distracting websites during work hours, or set designated times for checking emails or social media. Remember, you do what works for you.

CHAPTER III
BUILDING DILIGENT HABITS

Reward Yourself for Progress: Motivation can be maintained by rewarding yourself for completing tasks, especially challenging ones. Set up a reward system where you treat yourself to something small, like a favorite snack, a short break with a cup of coffee and a good conversation or an activity you enjoy after finishing a portion of your work. These small incentives help maintain focus and give you something to look forward to.

Visualize Success: Visualization is a powerful technique for staying motivated. Take a few moments to imagine the sense of accomplishment you'll feel once you complete the task. Picture how your work will positively impact your life or career. Visualizing the end result helps you stay focused and motivated, especially when the task feels difficult or tedious. For example: How can an Architect draw up a plan without a vision? Let's keep the momentum.

Adopt the Pomodoro Technique: The Pomodoro Technique is an **effective time-management** method that involves working in focused intervals (typically 25 minutes) followed by short breaks. By breaking work into timed sprints, you make tasks feel less daunting and create a sense of urgency. The frequent breaks also help maintain focus and prevent burnout.

CHAPTER III
BUILDING DILIGENT HABITS

Create a Productive Environment: Your work environment plays a big role in your ability to focus and avoid procrastination. Make sure your workspace is organized, comfortable, and free of distractions. A clean, well-lit environment can improve concentration and make it easier to stay on task.

Stay Connected to Your "Why": Staying motivated requires regularly reminding yourself why you're doing the work in the first place. Whether it's achieving long-term career goals, providing for your family, or personal fulfillment, keeping your larger purpose in mind will help you push through moments of procrastination. Write down your "why" and keep it visible to remind yourself of the importance of **"WHY"** you work hard.

These strategies can help you develop a strong work ethic, overcome procrastination, and stay motivated in both personal and professional pursuits. By adopting these habits and techniques, you'll find it easier to stay productive and focused on achieving your long-term goals.

CHAPTER IV
NAVIGATING CHALLENGES AND SETBACKS

1. Learning from Failures and Using Them as Opportunities for Growth

Why were mistakes in school treated as punishable offenses instead of chances for growth and learning? Just asking a question. Failure is often viewed negatively, but it can be one of the most powerful tools for personal and professional growth. Rather than seeing failure as the end of a journey, it's important to reframe it as an opportunity to learn, improve, and come back stronger. **Many successful individuals credit their greatest achievements to the lessons they learned from their failures.** Let's dive in. Here's how failure can be used as a stepping stone for growth.

CHAPTER IV
NAVIGATING CHALLENGES AND SETBACKS

1.1 Embrace Failure as a Learning Experience

One of the most important steps in learning from failure is changing your perspective. Instead of viewing failure as a reflection of your inadequacies, see it as a necessary part of the learning process. Each failure offers valuable insights into what went wrong and how to do better next time. For example, an entrepreneur who launches a business that doesn't succeed can learn critical lessons about market demand, customer behavior, and financial management, which they can apply to future ventures. **The best learning lessons comes through failing.**

1.2 Analyze What Went Wrong

Failure provides an opportunity for introspection and analysis. After experiencing a setback, it's essential to take the time to reflect on what led to the outcome. Was it a lack of preparation? Poor communication? Unrealistic expectations? By identifying the specific factors that contributed to failure, you gain the clarity needed to avoid making the same mistakes in the future. This process of reflection transforms failure into a learning tool, rather than a source of frustration. I can relate. **See things differently.**

CHAPTER IV
NAVIGATING CHALLENGES AND SETBACKS

1.3 Adjust Your Approach

Learning from failure often requires making adjustments. Once you've identified the causes of the failure, you can take steps to improve your methods or strategies. These adjustments might involve refining your goals, developing new skills, or seeking advice from mentors. Each failure can provide valuable feedback, guiding you toward a more effective approach the next time around. **You can't go the same way but expect a different result.**

1.4 Develop a Growth Mindset

A growth mindset is the belief that abilities and intelligence can be developed through effort and learning, rather than being fixed traits. **Embracing a growth mindset is essential for learning from failure.** People with this mindset view failure as a challenge to be overcome, not a dead end. They understand that setbacks are part of the journey toward success and that continuous improvement is possible with persistence and dedication. This mindset shifts the focus from dwelling on what went wrong to seeking solutions and learning from the experience.

CHAPTER IV
NAVIGATING CHALLENGES AND SETBACKS

1.5 Celebrate Small Wins Along the Way

It's important to remember that failure often occurs on the path to success, and it's not an isolated event. Learning from failure involves recognizing the progress made along the way. **Celebrate the small victories and improvements that result from overcoming setbacks.** This will keep you motivated and provide the confidence needed to continue moving forward, even after a failure.

1.6 Failure Builds Confidence and Resilience

Experiencing failure can build resilience and confidence over time. As you face setbacks and recover from them, you become more capable of handling future challenges. This resilience allows you to persevere even when things don't go as planned, and it equips you with the mental strength to push forward. Over time, you develop a stronger belief in your ability to overcome obstacles, which is essential for achieving long-term success.

CHAPTER IV
NAVIGATING CHALLENGES AND SETBACKS

2. Developing Resilience and Perseverance

Resilience and perseverance are crucial qualities that allow individuals to navigate life's inevitable challenges. They enable you to keep going, even when faced with adversity, setbacks, or failure. Developing these traits takes time and effort, but they are essential for personal growth and long-term success. Here are several strategies for cultivating resilience and perseverance.

2.1 Cultivate Emotional Awareness

Resilience starts with understanding and managing your emotions. When faced with failure or difficulty, it's natural to feel disappointed, frustrated, or even discouraged. However, being able to recognize these emotions and **deal with them in a healthy way is key** to developing resilience. Practice mindfulness or journaling to process your feelings and gain clarity. Emotional awareness helps you respond to setbacks with greater calm and focus, rather than being overwhelmed by negative emotions.

CHAPTER IV
NAVIGATING CHALLENGES AND SETBACKS

2.2 Maintain a Positive Outlook

A positive outlook is a vital component of resilience. This doesn't mean ignoring challenges or pretending everything is fine. Instead, it means believing in your ability to overcome difficulties and viewing obstacles as temporary. Optimism fosters perseverance because it helps you maintain hope and confidence in your ability to succeed, even in the face of setbacks. By focusing on solutions rather than problems, you create a mindset that encourages resilience.

2.3 Develop Problem-Solving Skills

Resilient people are proactive in addressing problems and finding solutions. When faced with a setback, instead of dwelling on what went wrong, they focus on how to fix it and move forward. Developing strong problem-solving skills will help you navigate challenges more effectively. Break down problems into smaller, more manageable parts, and tackle them step by step. This approach reduces the feeling of being overwhelmed and allows you to regain control of the situation.

CHAPTER IV
NAVIGATING CHALLENGES AND SETBACKS

2.4 Build a Support Network

Resilience is not a solo journey. Having a strong support network of friends, family, mentors, or colleagues can make a significant difference when dealing with challenges. Talking through your difficulties with others can provide new perspectives, solutions, and encouragement. Leaning on your support system during tough times doesn't make you weak — it demonstrates your willingness to seek help and grow.

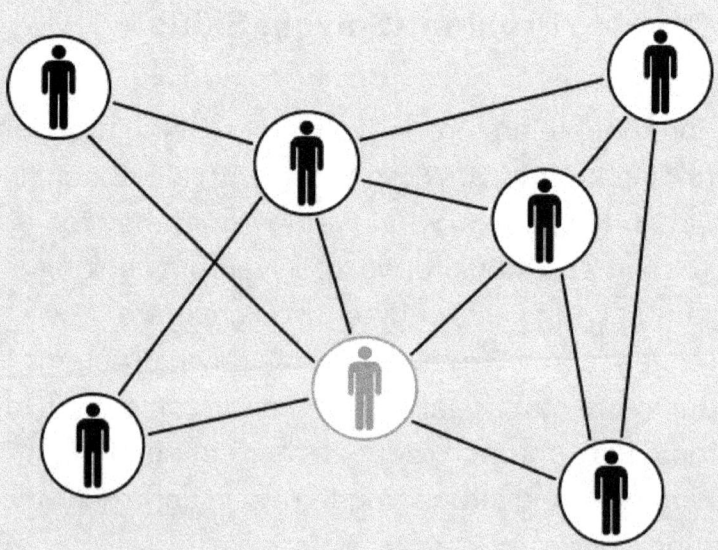

CHAPTER IV
NAVIGATING CHALLENGES AND SETBACKS
2.5 Set Long-Term Goals and Stay Focused

Perseverance is about staying focused on your long-term goals, even when the road gets tough. It's easy to give up when you don't see immediate results, but true perseverance requires patience and commitment. Set clear, realistic long-term goals and break them into smaller, achievable milestones. This gives you a sense of progress and makes the larger goal seem less daunting.

The key to perseverance is to keep your eyes on the ultimate outcome while making consistent progress along the way. I'm reminded of a long trip I did, where the ultimate goal was the destination. Although you can't see it yet, you press on, fueled by your purpose. Along the way, you'll need to take breaks and rest, but you can't lose sight of your objective or turn back, knowing that every step forward brings you closer to reaching your desired outcome.

CHAPTER IV
NAVIGATING CHALLENGES AND SETBACKS

2.6 Learn to Embrace Discomfort

Growth often happens outside of your comfort zone. Resilient individuals understand that discomfort is part of the process of improvement. Whether it's facing rejection, taking on new challenges, or pushing yourself to achieve difficult tasks, embracing discomfort helps you build mental toughness. **The more you practice stepping outside your comfort zone, the more you develop resilience and perseverance, preparing you for even greater challenges in the future.** In simple words: Keep doing what is uncomfortable and eventually it will become comfortable. What was once comfortable will now become uncomfortable.

2.7 Practice Self-Care and Stress Management

Resilience and perseverance are difficult to maintain if you're constantly feeling burnt out. **Prioritizing self-care is essential** to staying strong in the face of challenges. Make time for rest, physical activity, and activities that replenish your energy. Stress management techniques like meditation, deep breathing, or regular exercise can help you maintain mental and emotional balance. When you take care of your well-being, you're better equipped to handle adversity and bounce back from setbacks.

CHAPTER IV
NAVIGATING CHALLENGES AND SETBACKS

2.8 Focus on the Process, Not Just the Outcome

Finally, developing resilience and perseverance requires shifting your focus from the end result to the process itself. Instead of fixating solely on the goal, learn to appreciate the journey. **Each step you take, no matter how small, contributes to your overall growth and development.** By valuing the effort and learning that comes with every challenge, you'll be more likely to stick with your goals, even when progress seems slow or difficult.

By learning from failures and using them as opportunities for growth, while also developing resilience and perseverance, individuals can overcome obstacles and emerge stronger. These traits are essential for navigating life's challenges and achieving long-term success.

CHAPTER V
CULTIVATING A DILIGENT MINDSET

1. Understanding and Developing a Diligent Mindset

A diligent mindset is essential for achieving long-term success in both personal and professional areas of life. Diligence involves persistence, **careful attention to detail,** and the continuous effort to improve and complete tasks, no matter how challenging they may be. Cultivating a diligent mindset can be transformative, leading to greater productivity, growth, and fulfillment.

1.1 The Essence of a Diligent Mindset

At its core, diligence is about consistency and a proactive approach to handling responsibilities. A diligent person doesn't shy away from challenges or get easily discouraged when faced with obstacles. Instead, they approach their work methodically, putting in the necessary effort to meet their goals and stay on task. **Developing a diligent mindset means making a conscious decision to adopt this approach,** regardless of the difficulty or length of the journey.

CHAPTER V
CULTIVATING A DILIGENT MINDSET

1.2 The Power of Small Consistent Actions

A diligent mindset is not about working relentlessly without rest but about making steady, purposeful progress over time. Often, people think success comes from major, life-changing efforts. However, it's the small, consistent actions that build up to significant results. Committing to daily, focused work on a project or goal — whether it's learning a new skill, improving in your career, or working on personal habits — will lead to growth over time.

For example, a student who spends 30 minutes every day studying a subject will likely outperform a student who crams for exams at the last minute. This concept applies to all areas of life, from fitness to professional development. A diligent mindset requires recognizing the value of persistence, understanding that cumulative effort leads to success.

CHAPTER V
CULTIVATING A DILIGENT MINDSET

1.3 Setting Clear and Measurable Goals

Diligence is closely linked to having clear, measurable goals. Without goals, your efforts can feel aimless, and it becomes difficult to stay focused. Developing a diligent mindset involves setting specific objectives that guide your actions. Whether it's breaking down a large project into smaller milestones or creating a timeline for reaching personal goals, **clarity is key**. Once goals are in place, it's important to track progress and adjust as needed. This reflection allows you to see the fruits of your diligence, which can motivate you to continue working hard. Moreover, clear goals give you a sense of purpose, making the daily grind feel more meaningful.

CHAPTER V
CULTIVATING A DILIGENT MINDSET

1.4 Staying Motivated Through Challenges

Diligence requires maintaining motivation, even when facing setbacks or slow progress. When challenges arise, individuals with a diligent mindset push through, knowing that obstacles are a natural part of growth. Instead of being discouraged by setbacks, they see these moments as opportunities to learn and adapt. Maintaining a positive attitude, despite adversity, is essential in developing a mindset that thrives on hard work and perseverance.

One way to stay motivated is to remind yourself of your "why" — the reason behind your goals. Whether it's to achieve financial stability, improve health, or reach a career milestone, keeping the bigger picture in mind helps maintain focus during difficult times.

CHAPTER V
CULTIVATING A DILIGENT MINDSET

2. Practicing Self-Discipline and Self-Awareness

To sustain a diligent mindset, self-discipline and self-awareness are crucial. Both traits enable you to stay on track, resist distractions, and continually improve your personal and professional practices.

CHAPTER V
CULTIVATING A DILIGENT MINDSET

2.1 The Role of Self-Discipline

Self-discipline is the ability to control impulses and stay focused on long-term goals, even when faced with distractions, temptations, or immediate gratification. It is an essential ingredient in maintaining diligence over time. Self-discipline allows you to push past the natural urge to procrastinate, quit, or take the easy way out.

One of the most effective ways to develop self-discipline is by creating a structured routine. Having a consistent schedule helps reduce the mental fatigue that comes with decision-making and removes the temptation to stray from important tasks. For instance, setting aside dedicated time each day for important projects can help establish a pattern of work that eventually becomes a habit.

CHAPTER V
CULTIVATING A DILIGENT MINDSET

Another key to practicing self-discipline is setting boundaries. This might mean limiting distractions, such as social media or unproductive activities, during work hours. It could also involve creating personal boundaries, such as setting firm limits on work-life balance to avoid burnout. By developing strong self-discipline, you strengthen your ability to remain diligent, even when motivation wanes.

CHAPTER V
CULTIVATING A DILIGENT MINDSET

2.2 Building Self-Awareness

Self-awareness is the practice of understanding your thoughts, emotions, and behaviors, and how they impact your life. It plays a significant role in developing a diligent mindset because it helps you recognize patterns, identify areas for improvement, and adjust your actions accordingly. When you are self-aware, you can more easily identify when you are slipping into procrastination or when distractions are pulling you away from your goals.

To build self-awareness, regular reflection is important. This can be done through journaling, meditation, or simply taking time each day to think about your progress and the obstacles you've faced. By analyzing your actions and emotions, you gain insights into what motivates you, what drains your energy, and what distracts you from your goals. With this awareness, you can make intentional changes to your habits and thought processes, ensuring that you stay on the path to diligence.

CHAPTER V
CULTIVATING A DILIGENT MINDSET

2.3 Overcoming Internal Resistance

Internal resistance often arises when faced with difficult or uncomfortable tasks. This resistance can manifest as procrastination, avoidance, or negative self-talk. Practicing self-discipline and self-awareness helps you confront these mental barriers. When you feel resistance, self-awareness allows you to identify the cause — is it fear of failure, lack of interest, or feeling overwhelmed? Once identified, you can address the root issue.

For example, if you procrastinate because a task feels too big, you can break it down into smaller, more manageable steps. If negative self-talk is holding you back, practicing positive affirmations or seeking support from mentors can help you regain confidence. Overcoming internal resistance is a key aspect of both diligence and self-discipline.

CHAPTER V
CULTIVATING A DILIGENT MINDSET

2.4 Balancing Ambition with Self-Care

While diligence and self-discipline are important, it's also crucial to balance them with self-care. **Working relentlessly without rest can lead to burnout, which ultimately undermines productivity.** Self-discipline includes knowing when to take breaks and recharge. It involves managing your energy and ensuring that you are physically and mentally prepared to continue pursuing your goals.

Self-awareness helps you recognize when you need a break and when you're approaching burnout. By paying attention to your physical and emotional well-being, you can maintain a sustainable level of diligence over time. Incorporating regular rest, physical activity, and mindfulness practices into your routine ensures that you remain focused and energized.

CHAPTER V
CULTIVATING A DILIGENT MINDSET

In conclusion, understanding and developing a diligent mindset requires a combination of consistency, clear goal-setting, and the ability to stay motivated in the face of challenges. Practicing self-discipline and self-awareness further strengthens your ability to stay on track, resist distractions, and continually improve. Together, these qualities provide the foundation for long-term success in both personal and professional pursuits. There's so much more to say, for now stay blessed, take care and **remember to BE YOURSELF!**

SPECIAL THANKS

Firstly, I would like to thank God Almighty for giving me grace through His Son Jesus Christ.
To God be all the Glory and Honour.

I want to thank my beautiful family, wife and children for standing by my side.

This book was inspired by the (NIV) Bible verse Proverbs 10v4: LAZY HANDS MAKE A MAN POOR, BUT DILIGENT HANDS BRING WEALTH.

www.ingramcontent.com/pod-product-compliance
Lightning Source LLC
Chambersburg PA
CBHW070947220526
45471CB00007B/2924